If the Butte

A Transformational Journey
Through Self-Development

BY
DR. TRACIE M. DUNCAN

DEDICATION

I want to dedicate this book to God for creating me purposefully and to myself for finally believing in God.

Copyright © 2024 Tracie Duncan

All rights reserved.

No portion of this book may be reproduced in any form without written permission from the publisher or author except as permitted by U.S. copyright law.

TABLE OF CONTETNS

The Introduction is Critical 1

Understanding the roadmap 4

A Walk Through My Life 10

Attempted to Assassinate 14

Somethings Can Change Your Perspective 16

So, what is Love Anyway 17

Life Situations Can & Will Change You If You
Let It Good or Bad 19

Who Did I Become? 21

Really? Where Was I? 24

Remembering God 25

A Change 27

My Life Just Got Good 29

My Good Just Got Better 32

My Better Introduced Me to My Best 33

My Future is Still Flourishing 35

You Too Can Be Transformed 37

THE INTRODUCTION IS CRITICAL

Have you ever found yourself at a place where you cannot use your voice to convey Purpose within? What is the meaning of your life? Are you stranded by the hurt, pain, trauma, or disappointments that have taken place throughout your life's journey? This really does not apply to age because no matter what age we are, we all deal with it, and some carry it through their adult years. Making it difficult to discover one's Purpose and voice.

We have heard phrases like: "Let it go," "Get over it," "Don't dwell on the past," or ""Forgive them." We could only wish the process was as simple as the words that are spoken. However, no matter how hard you have tried, it still weighs on you from time to time, resurfacing at various stages of your life. Especially right when you arrive at a place of self-discovery. Better yet, you have had some great successes, but now that you are ready for the next level, you seem to be stuck, stagnated, and unable to move forward. However, you can overcome and take a journey to self-discovery, and this book will be your help and guide.

Let's pause and reflect. Ask yourself a few questions: What's roadblocks surface? Do you deal with things from your past or childhood? Do you feel inadequate? Do you seek validation? Someone to tell you you can do it. Another degree or certification? Or always looking for someone else to model yourself after. Oftentimes, we suppress the battles of life and try to quiet the noise or make it disappear with achievements or becoming what others said we could not. Suppression does not heal. It can cause false beliefs and build walls in various areas of your life. This can become a self protection mechanism, creating lies that you speak over your life, believing in negative and false affirmations, and quieting your voice as you move through life. Which results in you fighting against the natural process of life to be what God predestined you to become as you walk out on Purpose. Every experience in life adds to your building process, which allows you to speak positive truths over your life, allowing your voice to resound.

Listen, you are unique in yourself. The only you that God created. There is no model; this is the "First You" to do Life and Purpose as only you can! Your voice can be heard in a book, play, songs, speaking, leading, and influencing others. Come on, Sis, there will be no more holding back. Take this journey with me; you got this!

I have been where you are and have had many lessons learned. I lived the pure ugly, the uncertainty, and became the statistic, but with God, transformation took me from the ugly to beauty. From my good to better to my best! And Sis, I'm here to tell you that I am here to help you do the same!

This book is not a self-help book; it will be your start to a new or relieved Journey to self-discovery, identity, and understanding your Purpose; who God created you to be! Basically, it is a roadmap through your life. Where did it all start, where am I now, and where am I going to fulfill my voice today.

UNDERSTANDING THE ROADMAP

If the butterfly could speak, it would tell you there are patterns to life, and they reveal the Purpose God created you for; however, it comes with a process that you must go through and endure to be made.

In this book, as you read through my story, you will begin to look at the patterns in your life, dear butterfly. You can no longer stay silent. Staying silent does not allow you to arrive at Purpose. You will continue to go with the flow and accept other individuals' outlook on your life. The hardest experience in life will cause you to hide behind many different things, such as careers, people, relationships, spirituality, and more.

When you dig deep into your patterns throughout life, you can generally see how God has been working in your life all along. You will go through a phase of denial, a phase that says, "I have it all figured out," and one that says, "I have no idea what's going on with me." Warning may cause pain to surface; however, you must face your fears and accept your weaknesses to prevail. More questions may surface; give yourself grace and ask as many questions as needed. Here are a few to get the self-conversation started: Who am I? What am I doing with my life? Where am I going? When will I know my Purpose? What drives my passions? Why is my journey so hard? And how do I change the trajectory of my life?

Action Item:

The Direction of Purpose. The 5W's and H questions of life.

Let's Reflect: Take about 10 – 20 minutes to just really think about where you are currently in life. What area of your life do you want to Shift the most? When you look at the 5Ws and H questions above, what comes to mind?

Reflect & Write (this is preliminary):

Who?

What?

When?

Where?

Why?

How?

You must understand the ugliness of your life will always surface before the beauty. It's like the metamorphosis of a butterfly. A butterfly does not just bloom instantly into a beautiful creature with lovely, colorful wings. Delicate, bright, and rare. Living unbothered, flying about in its Purpose. It starts out as a small egg in a shell and then hatches into a caterpillar. Caterpillars have six tiny beadlike eyes on each side of their head above the strong upper jaws; they breathe through nine small openings on each side of their body, and their antennae are short. They are ugly, swarms and fury creatures, in my opinion, with no real purpose. But an amazing fact is they have as many as 4,000 muscles in their bodies. Side Note: People often have perceptions and cannot see what you are made of. Back to the caterpillar, all they do is eat. In the next phase, the caterpillar hides in a Chrysalis. It starts out soft, then hardens to form a protective shell. The Chrysalis hangs upside down from the cremaster until the butterfly is ready to evolve, emerging into an adult from the pupa. This is the final phase as the butterfly begins to reach the full peak of transformation; it turns into a fully emerged beautiful butterfly ready for its Life's Purpose.

This is how most of our lives can start, born as we are with all our unique features, some we like, some we do not. We start not knowing we have a purpose; we just go about life living, growing, learning, failing, and trying new things. We move from one phase of life to the next, often allowing life to define us by situations, experiences, and what we allow others to speak into our lives. Then we hang undefined, waiting in our Chrysalis. Sometimes, life makes us hard, and we become stuck and stagnated. There are also times when we make it to the full-grown beautiful butterfly and lose our focus on Purpose. Note: there is no age that defines when you will become the fully bloomed butterfly that will speak.

> There is no age that defines when you become the fully bloomed butterfly that will speak.

I can relate to the caterpillar and butterfly transformation because my life started very ugly. I started out as nothing, like the egg, then quickly emerged into an ugly caterpillar, thinking all hope was lost. This caused me to hide who I was and shy away from anything that would make me stand out. When I reflect on my life's journey with the 5Ws and H questions. I found that my childhood was the most traumatic time of my life. I mean, trying to understand the world as you grow is scary. Some parents do not believe children battle with real life problems. The Holy Bible tells us in John 10:10 that the thief comes to steal, kill, and destroy. The rest of that verse tells us, but Jesus came so we may live. So that same thief tries to assassinate your life young to destroy Purpose. God predestined us for Purpose Ephesians 1:5a.

Then, the thief tries to take us out during the teenage years. We are young and reckless with decisions, trying to figure out who we want to become; in our twenties, we are still discovering ourselves. By your mid-twenties to thirties, you are dealing with unresolved life issues as you grow, and by forty and beyond, you are supposed to be fully established according to some worldviews. However, this is not always the case when individuals have life trauma and turn of events at an earlier age. Note: you can't categorize God's timing of your life.

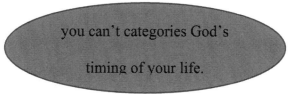

Each person has their own personalized journey, which must be endured to follow and succeed.

Action Item:

Let's Pause for Reflection…..Can you relate to anything you have read so far? Please Journal your thoughts.

You must start with you; no mentor, relatives; friends, etc. No one can tell you who you should be in life, but God, as you seek and pray for Him to reveal you as you go through this journey. You must own who God has created you to be and learn who that very person is today. Ask yourself a few more questions here:

1) How did I develop my belief system?

2) What shaped my worldviews?

3) What do I value?

4) How can I change my beliefs, worldviews, and values to better myself?

The discovery stage is the beginning of each step to reveal one's life journey. It reveals the truth that our lives have a purpose even in the most painful times; pain reveals Purpose, and problems lead us to solutions. Most often, we think no one understands where we are, where we have been; the mistakes and failures we have endured. I am here to share my personal journey from ugly to beautiful. I, too, was once the butterfly that could not speak. Only to discover my sole Purpose was to speak. The ugly did not destroy me. I am sharing to let you know you are unstoppable, and no matter where you are in life, you can go from Good to Better to your Best, living in and on Purpose with the ability to flourish into a beautiful butterfly that can speak. With God, all things are possible!

> **PAIN REVEAL'S PURPOSE AND PROBLEMS LEADS TO SOLUTIONS**

Along my life's journey God allowed me to understand and create a 7-Step Change Method to Succeed through my hardest life's journey. This method is built from the 7 days God created the earth; each day that He finished His work, He said, "It is Good." Even the power of words came from God Himself. So today, as you start this journey, speak words of good into your life. Listen, you "can" just say it without really believing. Just speak it until you believe; don't get discouraged. You can pray for God to help you increase your faith to believe; it can be developed, just keep working at it until you arrive. I did not learn this until I reached the end of my young life's journey in my late 30s. You can learn at any age; don't compare your stage and age; just know it's your time.

A WALK THROUGH MY LIFE

Life can change so suddenly, who knew it would change so fast for me and at such a very young age. My life changed at the age of 10 years old. I realized that my life was worth nothing and that my existence on earth did not have any purpose, value, or meaning. I know you're thinking, Wow, at 10 years old! How can you possibly feel this way? You are just a child who should be worrying about playing with dolls, school, friends, and favorite candies. Although you may be right, this was not the case for me; this was my reality.

I grew up in the heart of Detroit, on a beautiful neighborhood street and it was just migrating into a diverse community. We were the second or third African American Family to move on the block. I grew up with my mother, father, and grandparents in my life, along with eight siblings at the time. My mom had two girls pre-marriage to my dad, who had two children, one boy and one girl, pre-marriage of his own. After my parents got together, they had me and four more after me during this time in my life. Two more came later. Our house was always busy with a house full. I was the odd age child, right in the middle, and seemed to have nothing in common with my older or younger siblings, but I loved them dearly and loved to play with them; however, I often felt alone in a house full of people. I was the only child with glasses, and I had them since I was five years old. That was one thing that damaged my confidence, but to add to my problems, I was the only child with short hair (not so good either). I did not have long ponytails like the other girls, another factor that made me think I was super ugly. This is how my life begins to change (with a thought). You see, at 10 years old, you start to pay attention to how you look. I thought my problem list was full, but I discovered another major problem in my life at 10 years old…... .Hormones, hormones, hormones beyond what any 10-year-old child should ever experience. Yes, I started to have sexual urges very early on, but of course, I did not know what it was at the time, and it was scary. It made me feel that I was not a normal child, and I never talked to anyone about it, not one word.

So here I am, having a lot of things going on in my 10-year-old life and yet trying to just be a kid. More things began to take place. Yes, I know you think you had a mom and many sisters; why didn't you just talk to them, well another problem. I did not have the communicative type of family where you could have a heart-to-heart. Therefore, I thought I was a bad child and that it was all my fault that I was experiencing these problems. I started to notice and like boys. This was awkward for me because my friend at the time was a boy. Life really got weird when I started to think he was cute, oh my goodness, what was I to do? I had no clue, and although I had many sisters, I could not talk to them about it; they would make fun of me, right? So, I thought.

One day I was playing with my best friend, again he's a boy, and we loved to play sports together all the time, especially football. This particular day, I found myself thinking he was cute, and it would be nice if he liked me back; but he never looked at me as a cute girl. I was just his play buddy, just like another one of the boys, and that was all. He would say which girls were cute, and I would tease him about liking them, but I felt horrible on the inside. I had other friends on the block that were girls, and according to how I viewed things they were all pretty with long ponytails, especially my second-best friend. She also had every Barbie a girl could ever dream of, and she always shared them. Her grandmother would allow us to bake in her kitchen when we did not know a thing about it. The funny part is she never taught us. We would use many different ingredients and make a huge mess; they turned out pretty bad because we never ate them. We would try to sell them to the older boys across the street. We both thought they were very cute and would often giggle about it. Most people would say oh, that's just kids' stuff, nothing big, but for me, at 10 years old, it was huge! It was everything! Oh yeah, let me not leave out this classic story. When I was five years old, my dad took me to get glasses, and he allowed me to pick out my own. My mom was at home with the new baby. I picked out the pointiest glasses with rhinestones all around them and thought they were cute. When I got home, my mom was not happy. However, because of how the medical benefits worked back then, I could not take them back. So, from that day forth, I was talked about in a mean way and teased by everyone in my neighborhood, and even my siblings called me names like the gremlins and Ms. Beasley. And just when I thought things couldn't get worse, my hormones grew out of control, but I still stayed silent. I thought I was a terrible child for having such feelings, but I did not know what they were and why I was having them. Still, I never told anyone.

YOU MAY ASK YOURSELF AM I READING A CHILD'S BOOK? NO, BUT THESE ARE THE THINGS THAT SHAPE MY THINKING AT A VERY YOUNG AGE.

ATTEMPTED TO ASSASSINATE

One sunny day sitting in my backyard at the wooden picnic table across from the huge pool we had (before the storm slit it in half) with our mile-long backyard filled with very tall pine trees, I sat in sadness, thinking my life was horrible. I wrote a note saying I was the ugliest girl in the whole world, nobody loved me, and if I was not around, no one would miss me, so I was going to kill myself. You may ask yourself, how can a kid this young think this way? But it's very real; the devil's Job is to kill, steal, and destroy, and he wanted my life at a very early age, but God said, "No"! My dad walked into the backyard and asked me what I was writing about. I tried to hide it, but he saw it, took the paper, and read it; I was so ashamed. He looked at me and said Baby girl, this is silly because you are a very pretty girl, and you are going to be my lawyer one day. THE POWER OF WORDS! That statement gave me hope that I, too, could one day believe I was pretty and hoped others would be able to see it, too. Therefore, the devil's plan to end my life at 10 years old failed. However, I continued to battle thinking bad about myself and my hormonal issues. I was embarrassed for what I did not understand I was going through. However, a classmate of mine in the sixth grade shared a book with me called, "Dear God, It's Me, Margaret." This book blessed my life and helped me to understand the things I was dealing with and the changes my body was going through.

PAUSE!

SO, IF GOD GIVES YOU A STORY TO WRITE IN A BOOK TO SHARE, DON'T SIT ON IT. WRITE IT, IT JUST MIGHT CHANGE SOMEONE'S LIFE.

Okay, now where was I, oh yes because communication and information sharing were not known in my household; therefore, I suffered some things silently but discovered them in a book.

Summary

1. **My perspective was shaped by my negative thoughts**

2. **My lack of understanding gave me the wrong vision for my life**

3. **Not having influential people to communicate with left me on a path of endlessness**

SOMETHINGS CAN CHANGE YOUR PERSPECTIVE

As I grew older, I watched various television shows; one of my favorites was The Brady Bunch. This show was relatable; they had a big family with a lot of activity going on, but the thing I noticed was no matter the age the entire family interacted, talked, laughed, and did many things together as a family. This show made me ask God some questions. I wanted to know why the families on television only lived a good life. I wanted my big family to be a big, happy family that talked, played, took trips, and did everything together. I did not know I was young and naïve as I thought television was real life, but it gave me hope, and I was destined to find my own way.

SO, WHAT IS LOVE ANYWAY

As I grew older, I began to have misplaced feelings of what love was. I thought love was when you were pretty to someone else, so I would often daydream about my school crush at the time, hoping one day he would think I was pretty. I spent years trying to become pretty on the outside, seeking others approval to validate me as pretty and equating it with love. I NEVER KNEW I COULD DECLARE MYSELF TO BE PRETTY BECAUSE I NEVER BELIEVED IT. At this point in my life, I became a wayward teen following the wrong path in life at the age of 14. I watched with a close eye how the pretty girls dressed, walked, and talked and tried to model myself after them seeking to be someone I was not. I have now developed three major negative behaviors that would shape my world and impact my life and growth.

1. I DID NOT THINK MUCH OF MYSELF

2. I WAS ALWAYS SEEKING VALIDATION AND APPROVAL FROM OTHERS

3. I WAS TRYING TO BE SOMEONE I WAS NOT

This is a sure formula to anyone's self-destruction. This carried on with me throughout middle school, which was the next hardest three years of my life. I became a fighter out of anger. It was drawn out by my own negative attitude and dealing with people teasing and talking about me because I already believed the negative things about myself. It hurt even worse when others would say negative stuff, so I was already mad and ready to fight at the drop of a dime. In addition, I had a childhood bully who taunted me daily. This was not the kid I generally was, but it was the kid I quickly grew into. I was hiding behind the friendly, loving child. I was always ready to make friends and help people.

LIFE SITUATIONS CAN & WILL CHANGE YOU IF YOU LET IT GOOD OR BAD

I started to go through life trying to stay out of the way, believing I had no voice. I always tried to avoid conflict, but it always seemed to find me, and this taught me to stand up for myself by fighting. My childhood bully pushed me to the limit one day, and my anger caused me to stand up to my bully and fight back. She quickly came back with her big sister, ran behind me, and hit me in the eye with a rock. From that day forward, I promised myself no one would ever be able to bully me, and this drove me to become defensive and have a mouth out of this world.

By this time, my mom had changed her Life with Christ and started taking us to church at least three to four times a week, sometimes more. I was used to my grandfather taking us to church most Sundays, but not our parents. Mother Inez Williams was our church mother who was very powerful to us. When she spoke, it was as if you were talking to God. That's how much we, as a child, feared and respected her at the same time. I remember her telling me how much God loved me, and He just wanted to be a part of my life and wanted me to do good as a person. I will never forget that day she had all the youth in a class and taught us the Lord's Prayer. A seed was sown, but my life didn't change overnight.

By this time, I had hit my early teen years and high school. It quickly started out on the wrong path. I followed the wrong crowd and started to skip school, drink beer, and smoke cigarettes, but never really. I just wanted to blend in with others and become mature, so I followed my friends. Back then, we were able to go outside and play all day if we were on the block known as the street we lived on. My mom would call my siblings and me into the house mid-day and make us pray and read the Bible.

WHO DID I BECOME?

My mom and dad would get calls from the schools all the time for me fighting and getting kicked out. I was a handful, but only if I was being picked on first, and believe me, even the teachers were something else to deal with; I remember my driver education teacher tried to get "fresh" with me and put his hand on my leg, but I got him together and shortly after dropped out of the class. So, I built the belief system that my behavior was warned, and it did not phase me because they were wrong, and no one was going to stand up for me anyway.

It did not get better; I became attracted to older men. My older sister took me out of the house one night and took me to the bowling alley to hang out and then to an after-hour club. She was trying to meet up with a male friend of hers and did not want to go alone, so she dressed me up a little with jeans and a tight cut sleeveless sweater. I instantly felt mature from all the attention I got from the men. We made it to the after-hour club and I sat at a table by myself as she talked with her friend. A grown man came and asked me to slow dance, and I did. The smell of his cologne and his full beard was so attractive to me, I felt so grown up, and from that day forward, I was only interested in older men.

So now I had another problem, I WAS GROWING UP TOO FAST, before my time as the older generation would say. I had older aunts who started to take me to clubs and allowed me to dress older like them, they really trained me up in the way I should not go. They allowed me to drink and talk to older men. This took my attention completely away from school, and the more I realized I did not know the schoolwork, the more I would skip school. My aunts partied almost every day of the week. One of my aunts would let me use her identification to get into the clubs, they guys that worked the door did not pay any attention to the ID. I did a ton of clubbing during my teen years.

Finally, I lost my virginity in my teen years to a very popular older guy neighborhood, and boy, did I learn life early. He would be so loving, kind, and sweet. Always told me he never wanted to pressure me and so forth, but right afterward, I saw him with another older lady. I did not say anything; I just felt extremely stupid and cried my eyes out that night. This set me on another mission that was not good. I felt numb to emotions. I then dated another older man who changed my life. I felt my heart first, and whatever he said, I did with no hesitation. He played a major role in my life and taught me a lot; at this point, my life was spiraling out of control. All along, I had a mother, grandmother, and grandfather who stood in the gap for me and prayed over my life while I was out of control. My mom could not do much with me as I started to run away, BUT SHE NEVER STOPPED PRAYING. She put me in God's hand. My father and I relationship ended as he tried to beat the wrong out of me while doing his wrong. I moved in with an older girlfriend of mine that we grew up with and was very disappointed to see grown folk who did nothing with their lives day in and out. At this point in my life, I began to see how I was completely out of control. MANY SAID THERE WAS NO HOPE FOR ME.

SO NOW I HAVE ADDED MORE NEGATIVE BEHAVIORS TO MY LIFE:

1. DISOBEDIENT TO MY PARENTS

2. DISOBEDIENT TO God

3. GROWING UP TOO FAST

4. HANGING AROUND THE WRONG PEOPLE

REALLY? WHERE WAS I?

I had to stop and take a real look at where I had landed: I was not living in my parents' house. I was kicked out of school and could not get back in. My older boyfriend cheated on me, and I had friends who came against me and almost got gang-jumped over some lies, but God spared my life as someone stood in the gap and intervened. This all came crashing down. I had gotten to the point I wanted to take my life again. I realized I did not like any of the things I was doing. I never like to drink or smoke. I just want to blend in with others.

One night, I walked down to my grandmother's house; it was a little late, and a guy pulled up and started talking to me and offered me a ride. I said no thank you, then he offered to take me out to eat and told me I could drive. I said, "No," but then remembered how hungry I was with no money, so I changed my mind and went. He let me drive his car, took me out to eat, then raped me, and as I tried to get away, I could not. He told me tears don't mean anything and I better stop crying. He dropped me off back on my grandmother's street and if nothing ever happened. I never told anyone. I BLAMED MYSELF and grew colder with my emotions, and at that point in life, men and sex were just something to put a checkmark on. As I remember, my aunt said, "Men only want one thing, so don't believe in love."

ANOTHER NEGATIVE BEHAVIOR: ALLOWING OTHERS TO POUR NEGATIVELY INTO ME

REMEMBERING GOD

The next day, I walked down the same street, and I REMEMBERED GOD, I thought to myself, is this all life has to offer? Is this really what grown people do with their lives? I did not have a role model. I became a product of my environment, where all of this was all too common growing up. I remember saying, " I would never go to another church." Then I realized this was the life the devil had planned for me, Not God.

Then, I REMEMBERED GOD! After all my mixed emotions, I knew who to turn to for help. Proverbs 22:6 states, "Train up a child in the way they should go, and when they are older, they will not depart from the training." So, as I walked down my grandmother's street once again, I stopped, looked up to the sky, and said, God, please help me to be empowered. About ten minutes afterward, I remembered my mother telling me about Job Corp, which I told her I would never go to, but I called her immediately and had just a month before I turned 16 and told her I wanted to be enrolled. Job Corp was known for troubled teens and young adults who needed to get back on the right track with life, education, future careers, and learning a trade. This was a turning point in my life, and FOR THE FIRST TIME, I SAW A VISION FOR MY LIFE. My vision was that I, too, could be educated and become something more than I was, even when most people said there was no hope. This may sound simple to some, but for me, it was huge because I never thought I was smart. I missed out on a lot of schooling. Therefore, I always felt inadequate and would not speak up or ask questions.

THE MIND OF A CHILD, TEEN, AND EVEN YOUNG ADULTS ARE BUILT DIFFERENTLY THAN ADULTS, and what adults deem to be foolishness, simple, or just plain ole dumb can be life-altering for a young person. I wish I had learned this while raising my children, but I was too busy trying to find me while providing and raising them. I had my first child at 17, my second at 20, and my third at 24.

Job Corp blessed my life; I was not sure If I really liked it at first, and my mind was focused on my so-called friends at home and I wanted to go back. I went right back to the anger and fighting, but when I made it back home, I realized I was not missing anything, and people were doing the same old thing. I could not wait to go back to Job Corp after my break. I went back and CHANGED THE WAY I WAS THINKING. I then transferred from the nursing career trade to word processing class and loved it. 1. I got more interested in my general education and all the other benefits of the program. I graduated eight months later with a Word Processing Certification and went back home. I received my first Job and then got pregnant with my first child.

A CHANGE

Having a baby at such a young age woke me up, and I realized I didn't know much about anything. I knew how to take care of a baby because I had so many siblings, nieces, nephews, and cousins that I often babysat. All my friends had babies. This was during the big baby boom in the late 80s and early 90s. THIS IS WHEN I FIRST LEARNED THE POWER OF WORDS. I went to a temp agency and could not pass the test for a specific job. Although I learned how to type and do word processing. I still needed to further my education.

I was frustrated beyond measure, but I spoke out loud and said, " I will not be a welfare mom. I will be able to provide for my child whenever I need to; I will become something". I wanted more for myself and my child. By the time I truly believed this, I was pregnant with my second child. I went to Wayne County Community College and continued my journey of learning. I was blessed to connect with a teacher who showed me she cared and wanted to help me succeed. I finally felt like I could achieve something more because someone believed in me and was willing to show me they cared. I received a whole new level of commitment. I walked from my apartment to the college, which was about 15 minutes each way. I was pushing one child in a stroller and the second one on the way. After taking the initial test, I surprised myself with my level of knowledge. I had never fully applied myself or been taught how to apply myself. All IT TOOK

WAS FOR ONE PERSON TO BELIEVE IN ME TO PUSH ME TO SUCCEED.

The teacher stayed with me throughout my pregnancy and made a few house visits to ensure I finished well. God blessed me, and I passed my GED on the first try in all areas. This was a turning point in my life. I started to seek God's direction for my life.

MY LIFE JUST GOT GOOD

So now I am a single mom of two children, just completed my GED, and my perception has changed about myself and abilities. I felt like I could now live. I learned how to see a vision, I learned how to speak differently and positively for my life, and I learned how to talk to God. After achieving my GED, I quickly enrolled in business school, and it did not work out with my schedule and children. I made a few attempts but did not give up, and finally, God led me to the right school. I LEARNED TO NEVER GIVE UP AND ASK GOD FOR DIRECTIONS (You know if at first you don't succeed, try and try again). The school was called the Community Training and Development Center. This was a business school sponsored by IBM, and it was not your average school. This school introduced me to the real work world. On the day of orientation, the building was filled with hundreds of people, but by the time they finished telling us about the requirements of the school, there were not many left. This program was Monday through Friday, 8AM to 5:30 PM, with a 30-minute lunch. All the ladies had to wear professional dresses or skirts and blouses, flesh-tone stockings (I had never heard of flesh tone stockings), no big hair, no loud hair color, no piercing, not a lot of jewelry, and only two-inch heels. It also paid us a weekly stipend so we could have a bus fair and lunch money for the week. In addition to all that, they provided us with a clothing voucher to start our professional wardrobe off right; this was a great school for me.

1. I COULD SEE VISION AND BETTER FOR MYSELF AND FAMILY

2. I SPOKE BETTER FOR MY LIFE

3. I WANTED THIS FOR ME AND NOT TO BE LIKE SOMEONE ELSE

I Learned how to dress, speak, interact with others, and conduct myself professionally. Also, I learned how to be on time, even taking two buses to get there. I received a strong foundational structure of the real work world, an advanced Word Processing Certification, and learned every aspect of working in a business environment. I also learned how to seek employment, interview, and follow up. I was not nervous and had gained the confidence to talk with managers and not feel intimidated. This was an Awesome feeling.

After graduating from the program, I immediately applied for a Patient Registrar at a Hospital, and with persistence and follow-up with the hiring manager, I got my first professional Job. I had my own home, I got a car, and I was able to provide for my children. I FELT IMPORTANT TO ME AND MY CHILDREN. However, as I worked around more professional people, doctors, psychologists, social workers, nurses, clerical staff and more. I realized there was more to be achieved. I was able to learn and grow on the Job while training. I discovered I was a quick learner who could adapt quickly. WHEN I LOOKED AT OTHER PROFESSIONAL WOMEN, I DESIRED TO BE AS GOOD AS THEM FOR

MYSELF. I could now see myself achieving higher levels. I started to continuously seek knowledge and wisdom. THIS WAS THE START OF MY ONGOING SUCCESS; MY STORY HAD CHANGED.

MY GOOD JUST GOT BETTER

I had many more challenges and failures after this start, but learning the EmpowerMe 7-Step Model is what kept me going. I had my third child and went through the ups and downs of relationships, hanging with friends, and being comfortable with Everyday Life. I began to lose focus on continuously building myself, but I continuously grew on the Job. I learned how to build my experience to get better positions and jobs, but my mind was not career focused. I watched other people who worked with me go to nursing school, graduate, and become nurses. I watched my girlfriend's mom throughout my childhood and young adult life. Watching her achieve her educational goals, take care of her children, and change her life as she became a nurse inspired me to want more. Her life was my example and motivation. SO, REMEMBER, YOU NEVER KNOW WHO IS WATCHING YOUR LIFE, WHO YOU MAY BE INSPIRING WITH YOUR LIFE, SO LIVE OUT LOUD. This taught me not to limit myself and not to rely on my own knowledge.

MY BETTER INTRODUCED ME TO MY BEST

I had an encounter with God for myself. I was cleaning my children's room. I had both my daughters and was pregnant with my son at the time. God spoke to me and brought some old conversations to my memory. He said, "Do you remember you said you would give me your life when you became an adult? Remember you said you were too young to serve me in your teens. You said you had to achieve some lift goals before you would serve me, and I have provided that. Will you now serve me? I took a deep breath and truly remembered the conversations I previously had with God; I was in disbelief and said, "I did say all of that." THIS CREATED A MIND SHIFT, AND I STARTED MAKING CHANGES TO CHANGE MY LIFE. The EmpowerMe 7-Step Method flourished in my life.

1. I BEGAN TO *CREATE* VISION TO CHANGE MY LIFE'S DIRECTION

2. I BEGAN TO *SPEAK* VISION TO CHANGE TO ALL THAT WAS INVOLVED IN MY LIFE

3. I BEGAN TO *PUT THINGS IN PLACE*; I CHANGED MY MUSIC SELECTION AND CLOTHES (they were not good outside of work)

4. I BEGAN TO *PUT THINGS IN ORDER*; I INFORMED MY PARTYING FRIENDS THAT I WAS CHANGING

5. I STARTED TO *ESTABLISH* CHANGE IN MY LIFE; I FOUND A CHURCH HOME TO ATTEND WHERE I WOULD MAKE THE CHANGE

6. I HAD TO *EQUIP* MYSELF; I BROUGHT A BIBLE TO LEARN AND STARTED ATTENDING BIBLE STUDY

7. I **COMPLETED** CHANGE IN MY LIFE; I SURRENDERED MY ALL TO GOD, CONFESSED MY SINS, AND ASKED FOR FORGIVENESS AND A NEW LIFE IN CHRIST

I have heard many say the Bible stands for Basic Instruction Before Leaving Earth. However, through living and learning the Bible has shown me how to live and learn. It taught me the EmpowerMe 7-Step Change Model to Success, which I have used in all areas of my life. It taught me how to deal with emotions, how to overcome life challenges, how to live happy and healthy, how to grow great relationships and how to be happy in relationships when others don't want you to be; how to live on Purpose; how to be successful and become financially healthy. All while maintaining a real relationship with God, walking in obedience to His Word, living a life different than most, being good with being different, being whole, and not bound by my past.

MY FUTURE IS STILL FLOURISHING

LIFE WITH GOD IS POSSIBLE NO MATTER THE AGE OR STAGE OF YOUR LIFE. WE ALL HAVE A STORY!

God has continuously blessed, kept, and elevated me in my journey of life and continues to do so.

I have been blessed to have a great career path and educational journey. I have worked in many industries: Medical, Legal, Educational, Staffing, Automotive, Higher Learning, Spiritual, and Entrepreneurial and Utilities. God has blessed me from High School dropout to achieving an Associate of Applied Science in Business Administration, Bachelor of Applied Science in Management and Organizational Development, a Master of Business Administration, Generalized, and a Doctoral of Business Administration in Leadership, All-but-dissertation WITH GOD, ALL THINGS ARE POSSIBLE. I have taught leadership development and biblical courses. I have experience teaching collegiate courses in Operations Management and lean methodologies. I am John C. Maxwell, a Certified Speaker, Teacher, Trainer, and Coach. I have been the keynote speaker at various conferences, programs, and workshops. I am a lifelong learner who continues to educate myself to help others in my everyday life.

MY BEGINNING WAS NOT MY ENDING, BUT MY BEGINNING GAVE ME A BLESSED ENDING.

When a caterpillar goes through the metamorphosis of life, it never starts pretty; it's ugly, just as I thought of myself in the beginning, but the process that God created the caterpillar to go through is what gets it to the stage of full development and its true beauty.

TODAY, I AM A BUTTERFLY LIVING OUT MY TRUE BEAUTY AND PURPOSE TO EMPOWER OTHERS IN ALL AREAS OF THEIR LIFE BY BEING THE TRANSFORMATIONAL CHANGE AGENT THEY NEED TO GO THROUGH THEIR METAMORPHOSIS EXPERIENCE AND BY ADOPTING THE EMPOWERME7-STEP CHANGE MODEL TO SUCCEED AND FULLY DEVELOP IN THEIR UNIQUE BEAUTY

YOU TOO CAN BE TRANSFORMED

You may think reliving your story is painful, but it is real healing to your soul, a testimony to overcoming your story, a witness to help others, and a stepping stone to get you over your mountain and to your level of beauty. If you can't do it alone, there is always help. I am here for you::

Dr. Tracie Marie

Success@empowermeps.com

Praying for your healing and Life's Journey.

Fly Butterfly and Let Your Voice Be Heard!

Empowering you for a Lifetime, not for a Moment.

Made in the USA
Columbia, SC
07 February 2025

52809986R00024